Motherlode

RHAPSODY

Motherlode

RHAPSODY
61 Gainsborough Road,
Felixstowe, Suffolk IP11 7HS

ISBN 1 898030 35 9

Copyright © 2003 **Angela France for poems
and Elaine Blatchford for illustrations**
www.author.co.uk/france

The moral right of the author has been
asserted.

All rights reserved. No part of this publication
may be reproduced, stored in a retrieval
system, or transmitted, in any form or by any
means without the prior permission in
writing of Author Publishing Ltd.

This book is sold subject to the condition that
it shall not, by way of trade or otherwise, be
lent, resold, hired out or otherwise circulated
without the publisher's prior consent in any
form other than that supplied by the
publisher.

British Library Cataloguing in Publication
Data available.

Illustrations by Elaine Blatchford

Printed in Kent by JRDigital Print Services

Rhapsody is an imprint of Author Publishing Ltd

There's a part of every living thing that wants to become itself: the tadpole into the frog, the chrysalis into the butterfly, a damaged human being into a whole one. That is spirituality.

Ellen Bass

Poems

Albert 2
Badger Soul 4
Balance 5
Binge 6
Blue note 7
Broad Horizons 8
Tread soft 9
The time comes 10
Damson wine 11
Crickley Hill Mornings 12

Lessons from ammonites and beetles 16
Counting 18
Cut to the quick 19
Divine PMT 20
Dragons wait 21
Evening Flight 22
Flock Instinct 23
Goat love 24
Gorgon's Grief 26
Grave curiosity 27

Motherlode 31
Harlequin 32
Helicopters 33
Icarus moments 34
If I could sing 35
I Will 36
Leaving stones 38
January's lightening 39
Meeting Wild 40

Muscular Green Landlady 46
Moon cycle 47
Seasonal cliché 48

King's call 49
Half familiar 50
Mummers and Morris 51
Mornings' fall 52
November afternoons, 5pm 53
Listen 54
Philosophy Inaction 56
Lines of separation 57

Quiet histories 61
Iron memories 62
Repression 63
On finding a Prinknash Pottery jug 64
Philosophy v Topology 65
Waiting for Heaven 66
Wire dancing 67

Summer Fête 70
Taboo 72
The Gentry 74
The Leckhampton Stalwarts 75
The Old Ones wait 76
The Runner 77
Turning colours 78
Word sale 79

Shabby Goddess 83
Sonnet for Women 84
Small defences 85
Strip the Willow 86
Springtime 87
They said she'd have to kiss a lot of frogs 88
The Witch of Robinswood Hill 89
Tintagel 90
Treesong 91
Town views 92

Albert

He knows numbers, can
calculate to a shiny penny
the likely price of his veg and 'mums
as they break the hallowed ground
of his allotment, where neither weed
nor slug would dare intrude.
He never did, and never will, fathom
the mysteries of the words
on the page of the local Gazette,
pleas of "Grampy, read me a story"
lead to grumbling of lost spectacles
and denials that the ones on his head
will do.

He's never left the county, don't hold
with city folk. His bicycle, clattering and
squeaking to market, goes far enough for him.
He sees no sense in travel lest to sell
the onion strings hanging from his handlebars,
the leeks that sprout proud from his basket
and the bunches of 'mums, always some 'mums,
cradled in newspaper and tied with twine.

He shaves on Sundays 'cause he should
and drinks tea from the saucer for quick
cooling. He sleeps in his long-johns,
catches pigeons for the pot and thinks bread
and dripping fit supper for kings.

Yet he's a man who knows where
the elvers run, and how to hide
his carefully planted seeds
from the birds. He can tell how hard
the winter comes and where
the clouds will blow.

He knows how to coax a tree, with
wise pruning and soft care, to give
more fruit than it should and he knows
well how the earth gives back to those
who have given.

Badger Soul

This badger soul has waited
through dry years, hiding
in clear view.
Tending mysteries in deep soil
loam-rich with
contemplation.

Treading silent on worn paths,
guarding groves of secret growth.
Turning discoveries
with wary halts,
and pressing the find
into the warm earth wall
of the sanctuary sett;
making patterns to serve
the inward eye, while
they change and swirl
to the echo of thought

Balance

Silence collects in the deep hollow on the scarp
where trees strain through festooned layers of creeper
and last years leaves slowly desiccate to dust.

Distant noises of traffic and voices fade below the rim
and the Kestrels' thin keening dissipates in the scraps
of sky glimpsed between a lattice of still branches.

The bumps and curves of the hollow are bare;
the earth is powder-soft and dry. Nothing grows here
but the unreasonable trees that jealously guard the peace.

Time trickles and slows to a drip; quietness, like herbs,
heals in the right dose. A flap and clatter of pigeons' wings
as they startle from the tree top restores sweet balance.

Binge

I have overdosed on poetry,
she said,
leaning in the hallway and fanning
herself with the pastel programme.

Anxiously examining
my syntax for symptoms,
I wonder if I might break out
in rashes of iambs and trochees?

Might I stumble, dizzy
with rhyme, or see
my rising creative tension
climbing the tetrameter?

Or might I begin to
       break
my   lines
    in strange
        places?

Perhaps I had better take
a prose prophylactic.

Blue note

Turning like a sixpence on a blue note
the swirling purpled air makes
fallen leaves of hope.

Fallen leaves of hope too
fragile to withstand the singer whose
breath is scented with melancholy.

Scented with melancholy that condenses
heavy on curling skeletons which
with a whisper crumble to dust.

Crumble to dust as if an ancient
queen, freed from her sarcophagus,
could not survive the new adoration of now.

Broad Horizons

There are broader horizons
beyond these green hills;
where undulating savannas
stretch vision to disbelief,
where whispering dunes
meet boundless skies.

There are broader horizons
within these green hills;
in the particular dazzle
of the sun reflecting
from a wet holly leaf,
and in the silent, brief
perfection of a wood violet
growing in the bony fold
of an exposed root.

Tread soft

Tread soft the steps, to contentment's door
The way is slick with sharp trip wires crossed;
passage is not bought with wealth or lore.
Tread soft. The steps to contentment's door
Are not scaled by those who have forswore
Their love of life or have kindness lost.
Tread soft the steps to contentment's door,
The way is slick, with sharp trip wires crossed.

The time comes

Driven from oak groves
and from sacred stones that lurch
over forgotten hills,
they wait while

Time passes....

Resting in dusty vaulted roof,
smiling through leaf curls of stone.
Gilded and painted and set into glass
they wait, while

Time passes....

Weaving their wisdom into
the fabric of life,
in shadow and sunlight,
hiding in plain view
they wait, while

Time passes....

Patient as the stream delving
a canyon from a mountain.
Accepting whispered homage
in carved silence,
they wait, while

Time passes....

Damson wine

Cradled in candlelight,
stained glass glow tints fingertips
as if dipped in the ruby dapplings
on a stone church floor.

Feckless damson captured
in liquid garnet. Colour deep
as thought, summer rich
in careless fecundity.

Tasting the shadow
of horizon misted bloom
on blue black skin washes
summers end over my tongue
like salt.

Crickley Hill Mornings

My morning's glory to walk on Crickley Hill,
Carving space in my day both clear and fresh green.
My heart lifts with the soaring of sweet bird song
and my soul's greeting sings to the ancient trees.
I breathe in hope each morning with the clean air
while my step gladdens as if veiled in bridal white.

Mother Elder spreads her gown, frothy and white
as spring wakes the sleeping joy of Crickley Hill
The sense of new life carries on the clear air
and bluebells nod in glistening nests of green.
The catkins tremble soft on the hazel trees
and dawn brings ecstasy to the blackbird's song

Crickley blooms in full splendour with summer's song;
rabbits run, just a lightening glimpse of white.
Dappled shade dances under the spreading trees,
long grass bends in waves on the top of the hill,
the valley below, a tapestry of green
and the wild honeysuckle sweetens the air

Autumn blows in, bringing wood smoke on the air
while the sun's slow to rise, and late the bird's song.
Hips and haws scattered like jewels in the green,
mist in the valley a rolling sea of white.
Fire hued leaves rustle with each step on the hill
and squirrels scurry their bounty to the trees.

Winter walks in darkness 'neath moon silvered trees
clouds of misty breath hang silent on the air,
a fox trotting to her den under the hill
and the sounds of night creatures the only song.
Crisp underfoot, frosted grass gleams coldest white
while under the Beech, a brave snowdrop spikes green

Wherever I go, memory will be green,
season after season, I will greet the trees.
Whether there is autumn leaf or blossom white
I will still climb to taste the joy scented air
and hear the birds welcome the morning in song,
as dawn throws her mantle over Crickley Hill.

Earth Mother, wise and green, guard from harm your trees.
Sky Father, sing your song, keep clean your sweet air.
Let me dawn walk the hill till my hair is white

Lessons from ammonites and beetles

In my tenth summer, I sought ways
to clear my nostrils of the classroom smell,
and my mouth of the bitter taste
of casual playground cruelty. I played tag
with fantasy on the limestone hills;
I cherished the geography class knowledge
that it is Jurassic Limestone, that it's not a hill
but an Escarpment, and I felt that it heard
my knowledge and loved me for my understanding.

I scoured the old quarry workings for fossils,
pocketing ammonites and dreaming of
dinosaur bones, the discoveries that
could lift me to another world. I wove
stories from the shadows thrown by familiar
trees and the golden temple ruins of the stone
tramway pillars. Lying on my stomach
to tickle beetles with blades of grass and watch
them rear up, I thought myself Lilliputian
and envisioned saddles on stag beetles.

Mindful of the "Beware, Adders" signs, I trod
softly in the woods; not for fear but in hope
that I would overcome their shyness. Fortune smiled
on me by keeping them hidden; for they
would have naturally repaid my love for them
with venom, disregarding my dreams of communion.
'Til dusk drove me reluctantly homewards, I wandered
the scarp, peopling my worlds with miniature mammals
and giant insects. Spinning webs of intrigue in the scrub
and believing birds on the beauty of flight.

Parental concern about predators and perversions
brought a collie dog to my side, who became
another player on my stage, my confidante
and interpreter to yet other worlds. Little
did any of us know that I'd already met,
and been marked by, the dangers there. Years it was,
before I was to know that, something like an adder,
the habits of solitude and self-sufficiency hide
venom beneath their beauty.

Counting

Counting syllables on my fingers
Haiku eludes me; too many
years of stretching metaphor
and squeezing simile
just won't fit in to
a form that is
elegant
and so
small

Cut to the quick

The cutting runs deep behind the tidy houses, once
charged with rushing noise and hot metallic wind;
abandoned now, and blinded from its destination.

Down the matted bank, below pavement level
traffic sounds recede to another plane, crude steps
stumble beyond the crumbling brick wall.

The air is heavy and breathlessly still. Reaching
Sycamores touch leaves, arching over the path;
filtering the light to pale standing water green.

Elder and Hemlock, confident in their vigour,
squat stubbornly to narrow the track more each day
while nettles like acolytes cluster in their wake.

Tattered towers of Rosebay Willowherb rear
up the bank and lean into the tangled brambles,
oblivious to thorns and blessing them with petals.

The old bridge arches, dank into rubble; blooming
graffiti is gently faded by stealthy lichen and time.
In the stillness a lone leaf trembles and spins.

Divine PMT

It's not that great up here between
this mountain and its atmosphere:
dear Aphrodite still can preen
'cause she avoids bad hair. I fear
us lesser divines buy frizz-ease
in bulk and grow close to despair
with skin so dried by constant breeze,
no decent shops, fly-away hair.
The gods are boring with their talk
of smiting, fighting, cocks like trees
or worse: 'how many mortals walk
away from me weak at the knees'.
These idiots are wind and brawn
and ambrosia makes me yawn.

Dragons wait

Dragons wait in fifth dimension;
patient, in timeless suspension.
Man may find, if he doesn't learn
to share this world that he will earn
their unwanted, sharp attention.

Beyond man's poor comprehension,
yet too great for apprehension;
til time is ripe for their return,
dragons wait.

Still, they watch with rising tension;
brood on man's greed and dissention.
If man continues, earth to spurn,
he'll find it is his time to burn.
For re-birth in conflagration,
dragons wait.

Evening Flight

Swifts celebrate their evening
in arcs and swooping curves as they snatch
midges from the air. A tang of autumn that hangs
from the hedgerow sends them to gather
and twitter above; the habit of sky
cannot be denied and soon,
they will be gone.

Flock Instinct

Flocking on the street corner.
Iridescent colours of every hue,
twittering
and preening.
Their silent call
rings out:
Notice me!
Notice me!

Strutting in step.
Painted faces.
Each looking for the
right knight.
Watching each other
for the
wrong word,
wrong style,
wrong move.
Inwardly screaming
Don't notice me!
Don't notice me!

Goat love

If I were a goat
I could luxuriate in
the fumy rankness of the male's
self-urinated aura.
The dung between his toes
and the yellowing tangle
of his matted haunches
could only add
to his essential goatness
and make him sweet, to me.

And he, my cloven hoofed darling,
would not compare the brightness
of my slitty eye
or the lustre of my pelt
or the firmness of my udder
to other she-goats;
his interest would only be aroused
by the scent of a female
who is as ready,
and as female,
as she can be.

But I am not a goat, so
I am expected to rid
my legs of the hair that undulates,
silky on my inner calf and
wisps down-fair under my knee.
And say goodbye to the pert tufts
that make me smile when they
bristle like pirate's beards as I
curve my arm over my head to wash.

It seems I am supposed to colour
the grey in my hair, though every
strand is hard earned, and flatten
my soft belly though
I'd rather cradle it in my hands
and wonder at its impertinence.

In balancing my self against
supposeds and expecteds,
I would rather stay alone, unless
a lover happens by who
would savour the taste of me,
and not my soap.

Gorgon's Grief

There was a time, long since,
when my beauty was my pride.
Young men would cluster at my doorstep,
longing for a look and daring to hope for a kiss.

Now they haunt my threshold in sunny weather;
more like cherry-knocking boys than heroes,
thrusting their cleft chins forward to show
their beauty and pride: daring a look
and longing to offer the kiss of their steel.

I was lovely once; but they don't consider
how it feels to be desired only
as a means to prove bravery.
I ache for something warmer
than stone to touch.

Grave curiosity

Leaning and lichened memorials
cluster in forced intimacy.
Once cherished names, now forgotten,
lie down and coyly peep from
encroaching turf.

Yews in severity stand
between serenely weeping angels
and stones worn beyond identity.
On a high bank, under less cultured
trees a scatter of cracked slabs relax
into cow parsley.

What was it divided
Phillis Maria, Beloved daughter
or Also Elizabeth
from Thomas Henry, Beloved Son
to place him at the edge?

Was it act of charity or open purse
that brings Samson Pearn
to Enter Into Rest, laid straight
under the mullioned window
that frowns, wire defended,
from the church wall?

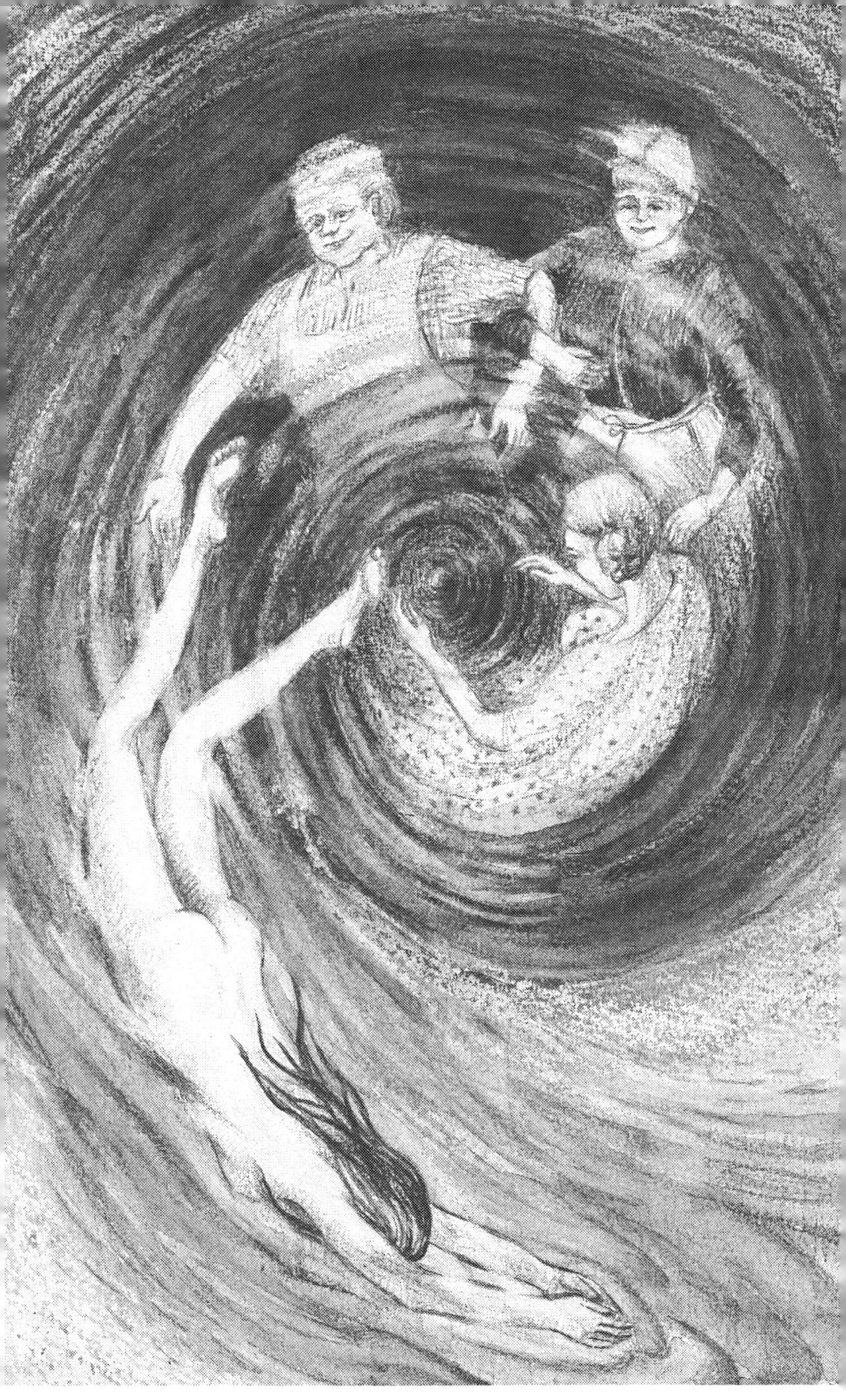

Motherlode

Ever present in the pitch of my voice,
always there in the shape of my bone,
women long gone show me my way.

They cluster knowingly behind my shoulders,
whispering tales of their lore to my ears
and slipping superstition under my skin.

Annie's weather-browned hand guides
while I dig and plant, the loam under her
fingernails calling to the earth under mine.

Over the cooking pots Nell always fusses,
nudging this herb or that into my sight
and muttering over potatoes cross cut.

The Elder blooms and Cunning Lil jabs
my ribs with her cackling elbow, gleeful
in sureness that old memories survive.

In the trees they rustle, watching the paths
whether strewn with rocks or smooth trod,
and when the wind blows, it calls Lucy to me.

They colour my blood and strengthen my bone,
they follow and lead me through the year's round
and each grey hair I grow brings me closer to
home.

Surely as rivers run down to the sea,
the women of my land run down in me.

Harlequin

Silently Harlequin
waits in the cloisters of
night. On the cusp of his
heartbreak the shadows of
hope leave him watching, and
helplessly waiting, for
She who'll not come to him.

Helicopters

We called them helicopters
and raced to see who could find
the one with the widest wings
on the seed, the one that would
spin longest in the air,
when twirled from our fingers.

Miss Sparrow said that each one made a helix
in the air as they fell from the tree,
but I never saw anything.
I looked hard for a helix
while my cousin and Davy Johnson
showed each other what they shouldn't.

I tried even harder to see one
when they said it was my turn,
and pretended that I couldn't hear.

Icarus moments

When Icarus flew
too close to the sun,
did he know a moment;
a twist in the gut,
a hammer to the heart,
a clench round the throat?
Did he have a sudden
realisation of dread
that in his soaring exultation
and his naive arrogance
he'd got it so terribly
wrong?

When Icarus fell
from the unforgiving sky,
tumbling and turning, did he;
berate himself,
kick himself,
chastise himself?
Did he come to the knowledge
that he'd ruined the
happiness he sought
by his own ambition
and pride?

Or when Icarus felt
his wings start to fail,
did he rage at injustice and;
blame his father,
blame the melting wax,
blame the feathers?
Did he blame
the sun for
shining?

If I could sing

If I could sing
I'd sing up a storm
of feeling,
croon under your skin
then open throated soar
until your heart leapt
to meet mine.

If I could dance
I'd dance to the moon
sway softly
for your eyes to fix on,
then spin whirling
till your dizzy heart
had to lean on mine.

If I could paint
I'd paint us a life
jewel coloured
to draw you like fire.
Then all else being grey
you'd stay by my side
and know
that the stars shine forever.

I Will

I will tread soft, at dawn
keeping my feet bare to feel
the earthsong. I will murmur
my needs to the between-times,
when dew glistens on filigree webs
and birds open their throats,
for joy, to the morning.

I will wash my hands and feet
in the spring that chuckles
down the mountain; and then
so tenderly cut the greenest
young rushes. One by one,
I will question their integrity;
selecting only the most true
and perfect spears to complement
my aims.

I will weave them with meadowsweet
and rosemary, winding two hairs; one
from you and one from me around
each stem. I will sing to the shape
of the basket as it forms between my
hands, and strengthen the handle by
braiding it with a hop bine while
I tuck forget-me-not in
every fold.

I will take the basket, and
your hand, at dusk; we will climb
to our glade to greet Old Man Willow.
We will place in the basket
pieces of our love and hang
it on an oak bough, then with
careful hands, plant a shiny leafed
vine in the soft leaf-mould below.

As the vine grows and winds to
bind the basket to the bough,
so will our love grow and bind
each to the other. As the basket
becomes hidden and safe from
all the world, so we will know
that whatever we do,
wherever we go,
there is a part of our love
kept safe, for our return.

Leaving stones

I have always picked up stones;

found on beaches and in woods,
in the playground where my child
played unaware, and on a friend's
patio when night and wine gave
illusions of meaning to talk.

I slipped stones into pockets
from a churchyard where confetti
blew to irritate carved angels
and from a house-plant pot
that accented the tidy room
of a sometimes lover.

Stones picked for their colour,
for a wink of embedded crystal
or for the comforting fit
of their curves to my hand.
Yet the years show that they dull,
whether piled in glass bowls
or arranged on a shelf.

I grow tired of their mute and dusty
reproachfulness, so walk out, these days,
with pockets bulging; not to weigh down,
but to lighten and to look for places
that would benefit from the leaving
of a stone.

January's lightening

In darkness Winter drags its feet, our hope
is hiding underground. The silhouette
of leafless woods, in silent pleading, grope
for warmth; their brittle twigs seem hopeless. Yet
so gradually early mornings lighten
as Dawn creeps further, stealing Night's dark time.
On Nature's scales the afternoons slow brighten
and trees are trembling, feeling Spring's sweet chime.
The Earth is undisturbed, but safe beneath
her secret face seeds quicken; life in threads
of creamy roots foretell the burst of leaf;
the season's nursed in Mother's loamy bed.
In subtle whispers, Spring calls "almost here":
her pledge renewed in ev'ry turning year.

Meeting Wild

"The woman, 52, spotted the panther-like creature in Church Road, Leckhampton" Gloucestershire Echo

A sharp and sudden stop of breath,
an alarm tremble in the chest,
at meeting wildness on an early morning
among polite red brick houses where
iron railings tame and contain
self-conscious reserves of long
grasses, so carefully selected for
the seduction of butterflies.

Did the primitive raising of fine hairs
and the tattoo of heart against ribs make
her want to run away, slipping and
stumbling to the safety of home?
Did she freeze and try to vanish
from the bore of those orange eyes?
Did her throat closing with fear
stifle the scream that was birthed
in her clenching stomach?

Or was her trembling the bone deep
knowledge of his essential being,
the yearning for the savannah sweetness
of his breath and the liquidly rippling
muscles under his light-swallowing pelt?

Did she hold her breath for fear that
the flame of his orange eye would turn
her way, or for fear that it wouldn't?

Did she tense against the slashing wound
that would, sure as the bite of glistening teeth,
sure as the rend of curved and cruel claw,
mark her for life?

Did she know that
long into her grey and mumbling years
she would whisper to herself "He looked
at me" while yearning for the fatal caress
of that heavy velvet paw.

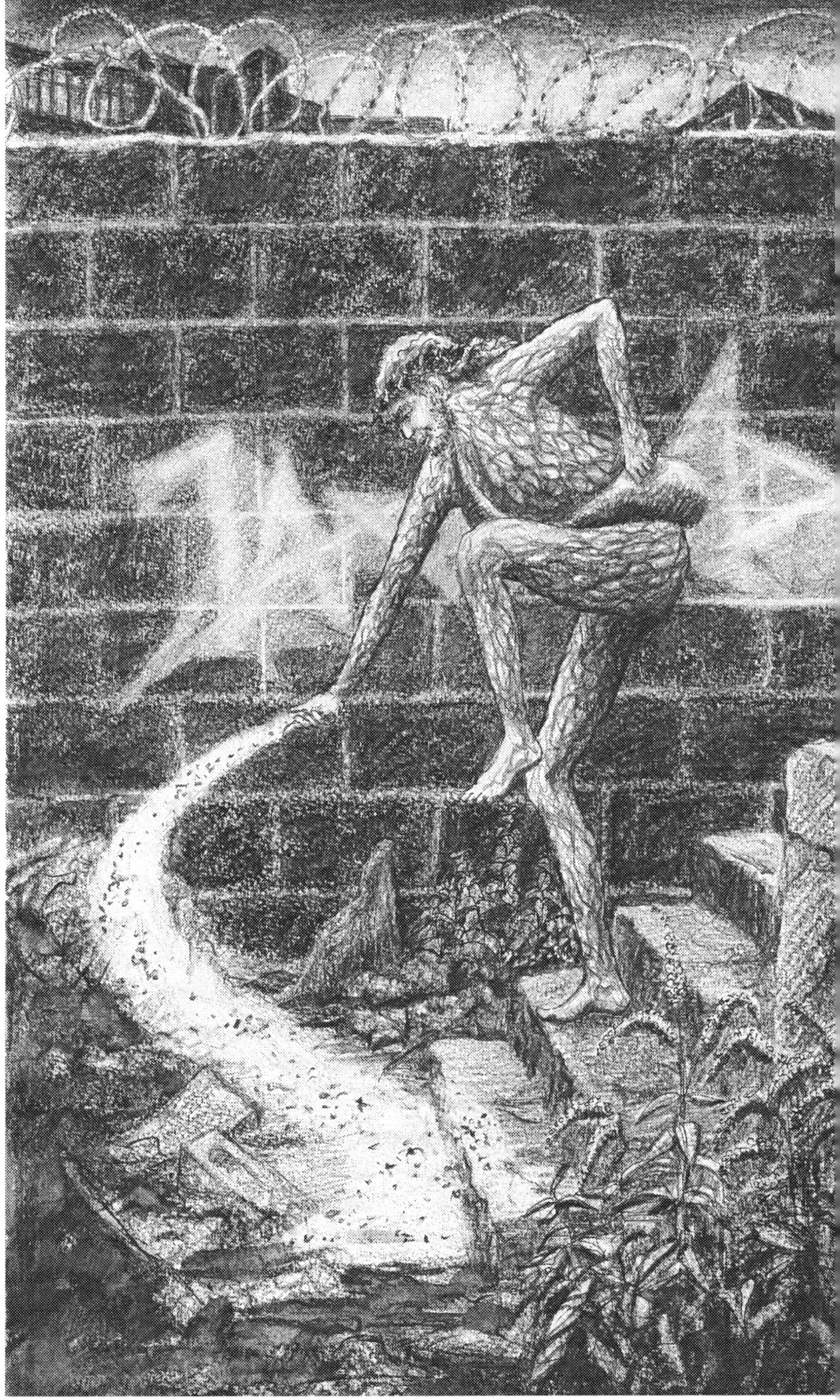

Muscular Green

Do not confine him to the
cliched woods; he lives beyond
the poetaster's vision of mossy trunk
and dappled shade where
ragged crow calls warning.

Tree born and copse secluded,
but his leafy gaze and hidden ear
will not neglect the city rat,
nor the lichens in dank sewers
that hum below the streets.

His sinewed thighs bestride
abandoned roofs to plant saplings
in choked gutters, while with clever
fingers he weaves beyond untangling
dog-rose into privet hedge and knits
their roots together.

He thrusts his seed to lie under
tarmac and concrete, his will
secreted into brick walls.
The smallest crack or crease
in defences lets his vanguard
through; delicate youngsters who
deny their green strength.

He may be captured by a chisel
but not held in the carving, stone
leaves serve only to keep him free.
He rests in dusty vaulted roofs
and clings to weathered spires.
Upright men who thought
to hide him only gave him
place and time to show,
He lives.

Landlady

She spreads her patched
and elderflower laced petticoats
to dip carelessly in the rivers,
and plumps her ample breasts
to make pillows for all who
come to crave comfort.

Her cheeks wrinkle with humour
as she teases and taunts with
a muddy cackle those who would
show off their Sunday bonnets.

Her deft brown fingers dig into soil,
planting and tending all that is green
and her throaty whisper calls me
from every tree.

Moon cycle

In my maiden years
I fought with the moon
as if she were a latin lover,
pitting my will against
the pull of her tides
for mastery of my months.

In motherhood, my girth grew
moon shaped in emulation
and in sisterhood I bent
my head in supplication
to the benevolence
of her power.

Now my body no longer
waxes and wanes to her bidding,
I can see that she was never
at mine. I ask nothing of her,
save to bathe in her impartial
silver light, and that when
my time comes she may bleach
my bones in her benign indifference.

Seasonal cliché

How should I not write of the colours
this year: when the exhaled breath
of the late, long summer has seared
all the hues and shades of flame
into cascades of leaves that shimmer
from gold to magenta in the last rays?

How could I not talk of the shining
copper drifts on the beech wood floor
that glimmer like a dragon's hoard
in the dew-dripped morning and the silent
strength of the spiders' webs that droop,
heavy with crystal beading?

How would I not mourn the quick
passing of another season when
this autumn fades more quickly
than the one before, while time
and gravity pile against me
like curled leaves under the trees?

King's call

Deep, deep we heard the call;
thrumming in the space
where sound and silence meet.
Sinew and muscle joined from sap,
we grew from the crevices in bark
and opened green eyes to our purpose.

To watch, and guard, the princely seed
is all our existence: the tree-length
of our gathering will shiver and reach
to startle any marauding squirrel or wasp.
We slither along the bough when wind
threatens to blow and stiffen along
leaf-veins to cradle the heir against falling.

Through the long season we stay alert
to any danger that may harm our prince;
our tireless eyes drinking his growth
until his time is come. Only then
can we gentle his drop with our breath
and cover him in his new bed.

Half familiar

Half familiar, that sideways look;
it tells of knowing beyond
the daily trail that bows
the head and numbs the senses.

The sharp dart of glittering eye
rakes the soul to watchfulness
and raises green shoots of memory
from overgrown fields of dreams.

Barely glimpsed in unlooked for places,
the compassionate curve of a tilted
head sounds a beacon call
to caves and crannies where
we hide from our deepest needs.

Seen in a lined and work worn face
or in the bold crow who stares where
others fly, felt in the clasp of a demented
hand and woven through the mumblings
of senility; like a shot to the heart,
it's there.

Mummers and Morris

It's Boxing Day, so gather together,
before the cathedral it's time to play
fiddles and flutes whatever the weather
for Mummers and Morris must have their day.

Take your sticks and your bells, hear the Squire say
"never forget your weskit of leather".
Clear heads from what was imbibed yesterday;
it's Boxing Day so gather together.

Come one, come all, come whosoever,
twelve noon and the Town Crier shouts "Oh Yea!"
The fiddler from his pint, we must sever,
before the cathedral it's time to play.

King George fights Robin and the people they
join the Doctor declaiming his blether.
In motley coats players bring, come what may,
fiddles and flutes whatever the weather.

The stone saints up high look like they never
had colour and noise to relieve their grey;
but music and dance are here forever
for Mummers and Morris must have their day.

Morris sides, come! dressed in your colours gay;
the music will play, don't wonder whether
Mummers will come to chase evil away.
They'll bring their old garb, to the last feather;
It's Boxing Day!

Mornings' fall

September mornings, everything droops
and bows to the scent of the ripened year.
Spindly docks arc, bent by the weight
of dew beading, and long grasses lie
flat as if tired from long standing.

The sky still colours a pretence of summer
but the slanted sun is slow to warm
and slow to dry the ground. A cascade
of creeper on the old pine drips
seeds, their filigree clumped by dowsing.

Mornings fall heavy on aging years
and all movement creaks with the burden,
but blazes of red and obsidian black startle
between fading leaves: sustenance
for the void ahead, bright points
on a circle not an end.

November afternoons, 5pm

November afternoons, night creeps early;
chasing from corners the lightness of day,
the street lamps glow is yellow and surly.

Wet pavements reflect what the sky won't say,
and between the lamps the shadows gather
chasing from corners the lightness of day.

Houses show closed faces to the weather,
weary workers yearn for hearth and hot food,
and between the lamps the shadows gather.

The heavy sky shows the month's sullen mood,
lovers plan firelight behind solid doors;
weary workers yearn for hearth and hot food.

Cats wait on doorsteps with inward tucked paws,
windows glow welcome where someone is home;
lovers plan firelight behind solid doors.

Children out from school don't tarry or roam,
windows glow welcome where someone is home.
November afternoons, night creeps early;
the street lamps glow is yellow and surly.

Listen

Can you hear the earth-sounds?
Can you hear grains of soil
moving as a seed sprouts a root?
Or, under the creak of a glacier,
can you hear the
groan of pressure as gems
are forged, deep below?

Can you hear the air-sounds?
Can you hear oxygen creeping
through a leaf's capillaries?
Or, under the wind's howl,
can you hear grains of sand
being dropped to make new dunes?

Can you hear the water-sounds?
Can you hear the dew forming
on each strand of a spider's web?
Or, under a rushing river,
can you hear the patient friction
that deepens a canyon through an age?

Can you hear the fire-sounds?
Can you hear the white hot breath
of the magma far beneath our feet?
Or, under the roar of a forest fire,
can you hear the pop of a seed
pod exploding to make new life?

Can you hear the sounds
of marching feet on a sandy road?
Can you hear the whisper of
a war head being polished or
the soft drip of oil on machinery?

Can you hear the sounds
of the loom swishing as the
winding sheets are made?
Can you hear the sounds
of the gravediggers spade as it
bites into the earth?
Can you hear the sounds
of the universe, weeping?

Philosophy Inaction

He seduced her with philosophy,
caressed her with discussions
of ethics and dropped
polysyllabic words
at her feet like petals.

He tempted her with determinism
while discoursing on Descartes.
Moving on, she found it hard
to resist scepticism
so lovingly presented. He told
her he admired her mind
while tracing, with his finger,
how utilitarian the development
of act to rule, and stroking
his admiration for Stuart-Mill.

A melding of intellects,
a meeting of fine minds,
yet she found his Act too
Utilitarian and wished
she hadn't sent away single
syllable Joe.

Lines of separation

Her pale back curves a smile
between t-shirt and jeans
as she stretches to a high shelf;
unconscious of her grace
and forgetful of the lovingly
drawn black lines that
slip from their cover
to startle and challenge
her mother's view.

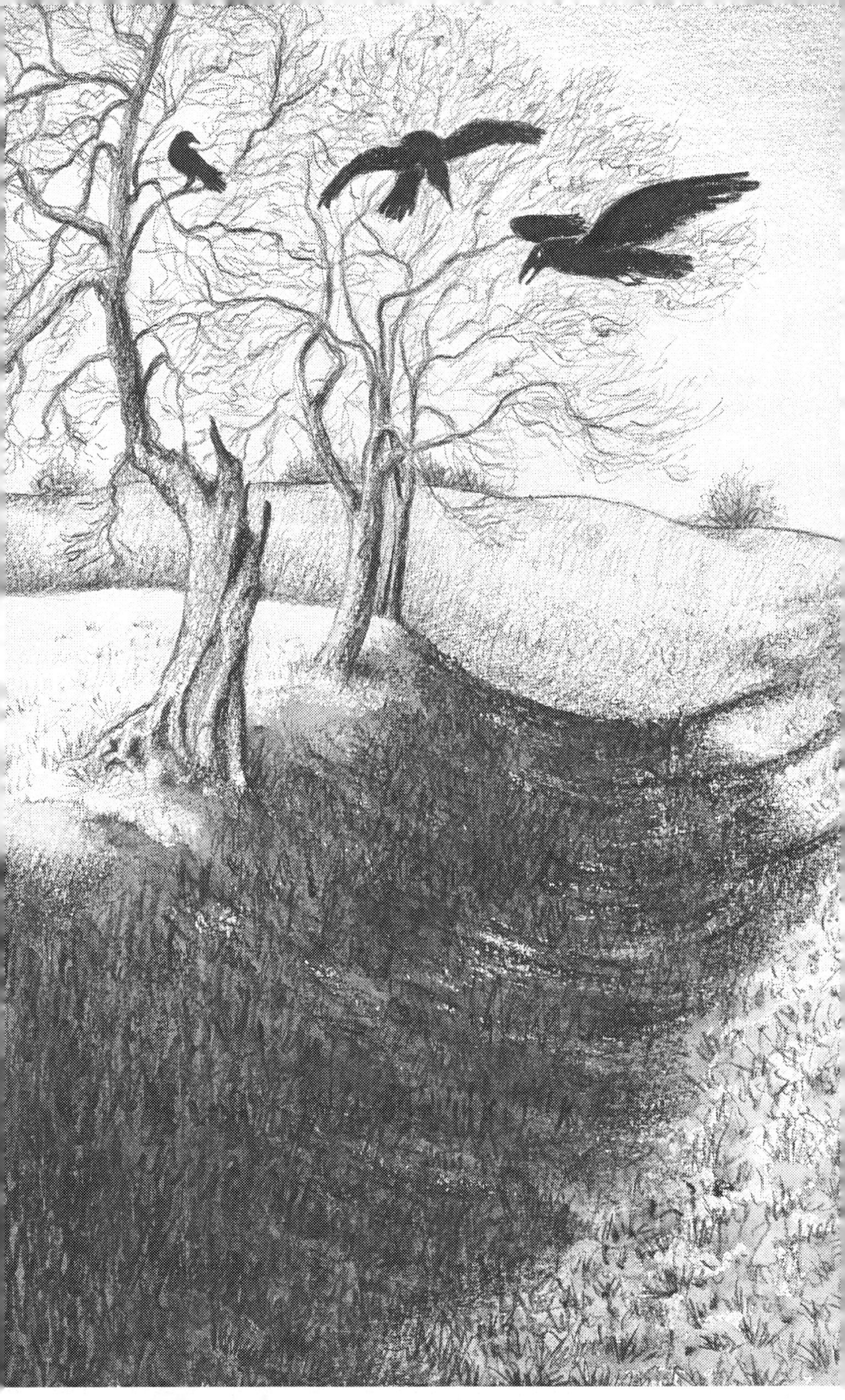

Quiet histories

There are quieter histories
than those that blast from chalk hills
where long man stands proud
and white horse canters;
and those trumpeted by giant
henge stones from
the postcards and pictures
that proliferate like the rabbits
on the limpid downs.

There are more discreet histories
than those packaged and mown
behind fences; where glossy
leaflets instruct visitors which way
to walk and how to see, where
senses are tricked into deafness
by lessons and explanations
packaged for popularity
and meted out on laminated boards.

There are retiring green hollows
where leaning stones and long
barrows murmur their stories
in whispers under sound;
where a sense of long passed
rituals and peoples reverberate
through trembling leaf and scaly
root. There are trees with no names,
whose great age is beyond counting,
that croon bass histories to fill
thirsting senses.

Iron memories

Scrubby young trees crowd against
the base of the earthworks, coveting
the space as the Romans once did.
Spills of raw earth tell of new rabbit
burrows, brave now that arrows don't fly.
Their young nesting deep in the barrow,
indifferent to artefacts crowding their bed.
Faded signs give history in snatches, small bites
meted out at family picnics as toys.

Yet at dawn when the high plateau is lonely,
shadows and whispers tease the margins
of sense; a halt in the breeze suggests
a shimmer of roundhouse and long grass bends
before a sickle unseen. Only the wind is there
for the hearing, but dog barks and voices resound
in the head. A flash of brown bodies, the chink
of a flint fall, the vibrations of chants round
the spirit-mans web. A cry of alarm, fleeting
shades on the scarp, a clatter of weapons
and the crackle and glimmer of fire all around.

Sudden, a silent moment as the blackest
of crows alights on a branch. Raucous he calls,
tilting his head, his darkling eye bright sharpens
over the ground. Nothing remains but mounds
and hollows; yet the earth remembers all that are gone.

Repression

The division of earphones define today's loyalties
as they jiggle and elbow around the mirror at break.
Safiya tucks the wire in with her hair as she dances

and only her eyes show that she smiles. She sings
the same songs, but they can't see her lip-sync:
sometimes she wishes they could see her teeth gleam.

The girls flirt and posture in branded clothes and tattooed
skin: warily like stiff legged dogs they watch, as in shifts
and circles, the groupings change. Checking their armour

for cracks they try and trade make up, Safiya adjusts
her hajib and refuses the lipstick but giggles as they sample
her kohl. She knows her eyes are lovely above the veil.

On finding a Prinknash Pottery jug

A simple jug,
glazed opal deep
graphite dark.

It holds a hillside where an Abbey kneels
among trees, and men in kilted robes tend herbs.

Reflecting
contemplative hands,
stained red in clay.

Within, a valley that bowls down to a river,
hedgerow-stitched in shades and shadows of
green.

Moulded to shape
by fingers
of strong grace.

It contains a sky that dips to touch the hills;
the challenge of silence for the unquiet mind.

Philosophy v Topology

Through long nights they flexed
their vocabularies in discussions
as circular as the red wine stains
their tumblers left on the bed-side table.

He wore his nihilism like a shroud
and used his existential despair to shade
the view from their small window
while she countered with exhortations
to anarchy that made her glow
with bleak fire through her limbs.

They defended their high room
from capitalism with swords of squalor
and stood together against the secret shame
of their Middle England families.
They marched with joined hands and philosophy
on their banners but, in the end, they couldn't
reconcile their topology:

He saw life as a helix, pointlessly
circling around the same place while
relentlessly driven down to the grave,
and she saw experience as a Möbius strip
that brought her back to the same spot
from a different viewpoint each time.

Waiting for Heaven

Fading palm crosses ranged in line
measure her Easters. Hope to brace
against the greyness of her face;
flimsy struts to prop a tired spine,
snake oil steps towards the divine.
Life sacrificed to ought and should,
loneliness wrought by being good.
She always worked to do her duty
for a promise of death's beauty
while heaven was there: where she stood.

Wire dancing

Dancing on the wire,
twirling and turning,
to the drumming wind's
demand.
Perpetual motion
with no choice or will.

Tied to each other,
tied to the moment when
they flew; exuberant arc,
weightless seconds,
captured by wire.

A moment of release,
of escape from books
and blackboards, from
homework and grades;
throwing gym shoes high
to salute the summer ahead.
Or...

A moment of fear,
Jostling and shouting;
an alpha showing his power
to omegas, taking a trophy
and swinging it high.
Running and hooting
as hopeless eyes look on.

Twirling and turning,
tied to the wire,
tied to the moment,
and dancing.

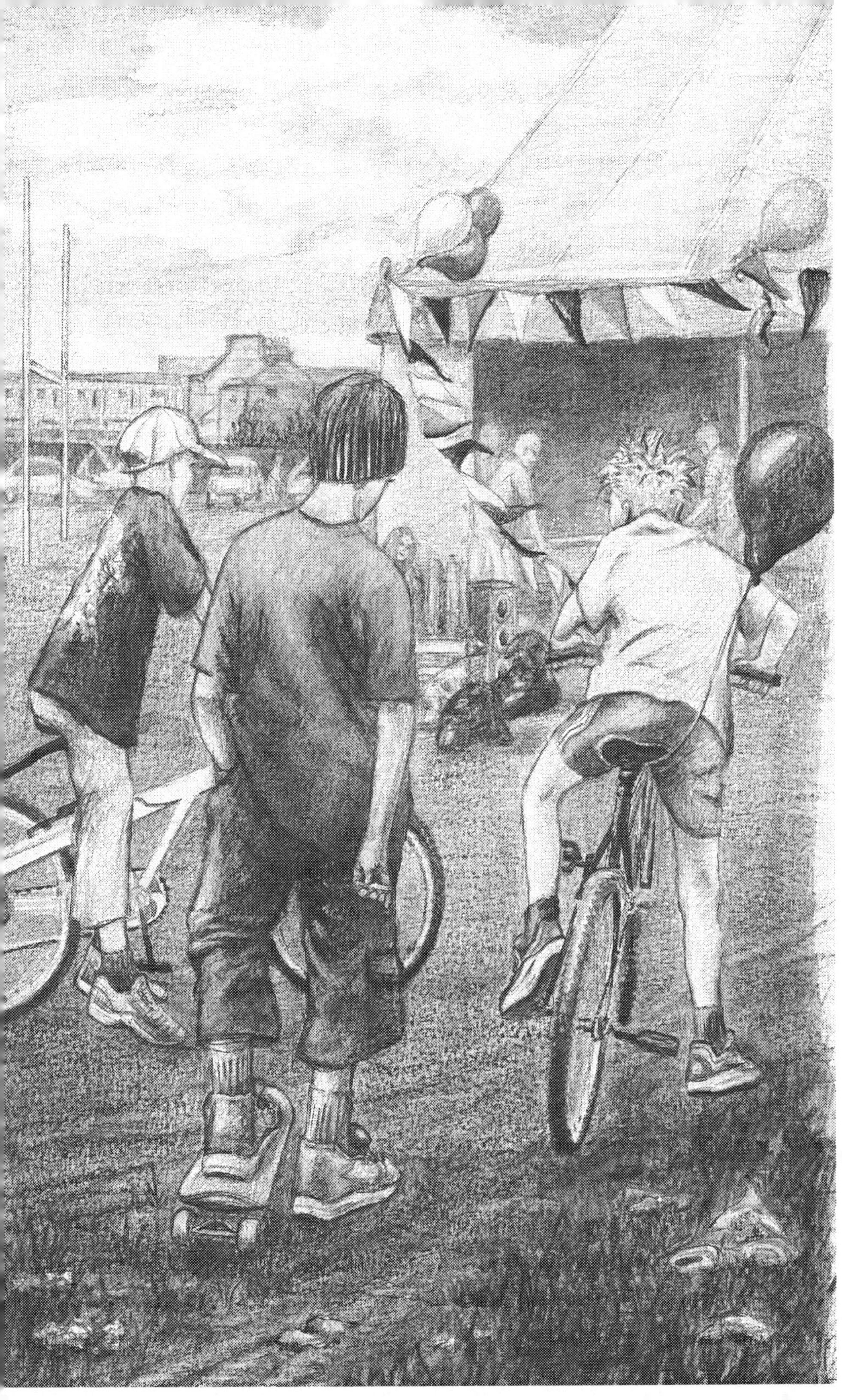

Summer Fête

No strawberries at this fete,
no floral skirts or home made jam.
But the community project workers
have borrowed a marquee, wrestling with
unfamiliar poles and hauling on canvas
that flaps in the wind as they worry
to each other "will the weather hold?"
Squawks and crackles from
the borrowed P.A. and it's open;
no celebrity nor vicar declaring it so,
just the queue at the gate swarming in.

So they come, first the young bloods
with skateboard under arm or holding
the handlebars of their low slung, high
sprung bikes. New knights on aluminium
steeds, jousting with postures and looks.
The girls totter in small flocks, tender faces
tilting to the best chance while their bare
arms shiver in the wind.

Local radio's flame painted jeep is here,
its bright shiny people wearing matching
tee shirts and smiles while the power leads
through the rugby club window blow fuses
with each new demand. The tombola's set out,
where cynical teddies jostle for space
with cheap wine and the stall holders worry
"will the weather hold?"

Mothers and grannies elbow for bargains while
children get sticky with sugary things. The core
of the neighbourhood is here to see; morals,
and pairings, picked over like bones.
The bar's serving beer, and gypsy-dark dads
escape face-painted toddlers for the respite
it gives. Terriers strain on leads to snarl
at each other, showing their teeth like
the young men they're with. Ebbing and flowing,
the crowd circle the centre where the tug-of-war's
won by the drug workers team.

The afternoon fades, and the rain has held off,
mothers and children drag tired towards home.
The raffles been drawn, the toy stall is empty,
the burgers and hot dogs sold off at half price.
Detritus from half a day's dream blows against
fences as the grey streets swallow the families
whole. Only the boys with their bikes linger,
watching the workers take everything down.
Young hyenas sharp to scavenge small pickings;
hungry for life beyond the mean chances
they've seen.

Taboo

To speak of such things
in the company
of those who stop their ears
with platitudes
and baffle their hearts in quilting,
is to hold a golden snake's eye
in the hand
and scent the flicker
of its ruby tongue.

To speak of such things
with those who would live
in muffled quietude,
minds insulated from thought
with eiderdown,
is to trace, with the stamen
of a snowdrop, amber spots
on the belly of a crested newt.

To speak of such things
to those who bind their senses
with straightjackets of denial
and smooth their wrinkles
with honeyed words,
is to follow the trail of a butterfly
by the air its wings displaced
and the sweet odour of its breath.

To speak of such things
to those with hearts and minds
unguarded to hear,
is to release from the slime
of a stagnant pool
silver bubbles of clean air
that will rise
unexpected in the sunlight.

It is to release from hood and jesses
a once-wild eagle that will soar
to the open sky and glide
with joy in its wings.

The Gentry

Be careful of the Guardians there,
in the stone circle take great care
where by the stones you place your feet.
Step soft and sure lest you should meet
the Gentry, perilous and fair.

Feel the tremble upon the air;
speak in whispers and stay aware
of whose ground will feel your heartbeat.
Be careful.

Do not name them here, or else bear
the keen touch of their sapphire stare.
Lords and Ladies you cannot cheat;
if once called, though they're so discreet,
their presence they will sure declare.
Be careful…

The Leckhampton Stalwarts

My Da's Granda played in that pit,
the bosses, they don't care one whit.
Our few rest days they want to kill;
but brothers! They'll not take our hill!

The quarry bosses rule our lives;
they make old women of our wives.
Our children grow weakly and ill
but brothers! They'll not take our hill!

They take our sweat, our blood and breath;
they work us to the ground til death.
They'll grind us down and break our will,
but brothers! They'll not take our hill!

They built a house to block our way;
we'll tear it down by end of day.
Two thousand strong with blood to spill;
but brothers! They'll not take our hill!

You stalwart men of Leckhampton
we must fight on 'til rights are won.
Whate'er they build, we'll raze it still,
but brothers! They'll not take our hill!

Leckhampton Hill, as well as once providing employment in its quarries, has been used for recreation by the local people for centuries. In the late 19th century, the quarry owner started blocking footpaths and rights of way to the hill, incensing local workers when he built a cottage at the foot of the hill in a gravel pit that was used for fairs and holidays. The peoples' protests became a riot and the cottage was razed to the ground. The leaders of the protests, known as 'The Leckhampton Stalwarts', all served prison sentences. Today, the hill is free and open to the local people.

The Old Ones wait

We are still here,
dark fire yet runs in our veins
though, for lack of calling,
it moves sluggish and sleepy
like a worker's rest-day afternoon.

Scrunched into eroding stone,
we round our shoulders to fit
into worn menhirs and lie
in dark cairns. We crowd in forests
where the need for sympathetic space
outweighs pantheonic rivalries.

Sustained by the old places,
we also lie under your constructed
emptiness; sliding beneath the tarmac
and watching the concrete
for the cracks to show.

We whisper to inform
your language and charge
your destinations with meaning.
The young and the old hear
us in the stillness of their fears.

We still tend the turning of the year,
and will see it turn still
when our names are gone
from memory.

The Runner

Seeing a man running up the hill,
imagining middle-aged spread
turned to mature muscle:
thinking of lean brown replacing
cellulite white. Speculating on
the benefits to my grateful heart.

Seeing a man running up the hill,
and considering the redness
of his sweat-drenched face;
imagining the pounding of heart
and the desperate sucking of lungs
for air. Thinking of the trembling
that besets tired legs and the deep
ache of overused muscle.

Seeing a man running up the hill,
knowing how the roar of pounding
blood in his ears will deafen him
to birdsong; speculating how
the concentration of forcing one foot
in front of the other will blind him
to the wild violet that hides behind
a tree root and how the sweat in his
eyes will blur the riotous green of
new leaves. Deciding that,
on the whole, I'd rather
stay unfit.

Turning colours

All colours of lupins,
they say, will turn blue
if left alone
without cultivation
or fertilisation.

If I were left
without cultivation
or expectation,
I could turn
sky coloured
and water scented.

I could haunt the woods,
badger striped
and grass stained,
to feed on bird song.

I could open my pores
to let the wind
trickle under my skin
and rest in the arms
of the old oak
with wild contentment
for my pillow.

Word sale

I cannot rest while my bed is gritty with
consonants and my pillow is lumpy with vowels.
There is no hope of sleep while a hundred
monkeys chatter over their typewriters between
my ears and their scrunched paper crackles
and scratches at the back of my throat.

If I could empty my head of words and sort them
into washed jam jars, I would sell them for a penny
an ounce and advertise a glue stick included, free.

Ideal Rainy Day Occupation or Perfect for Long Journeys.
Some entrepreneur could make a Dentist Waiting Room kit
or a pack for use in the car, with built-in equilibrium
to counter motion sickness.

They would be delivered promptly, with no guarantee
of poetry, and no return address: only my thanks,
for sleep.

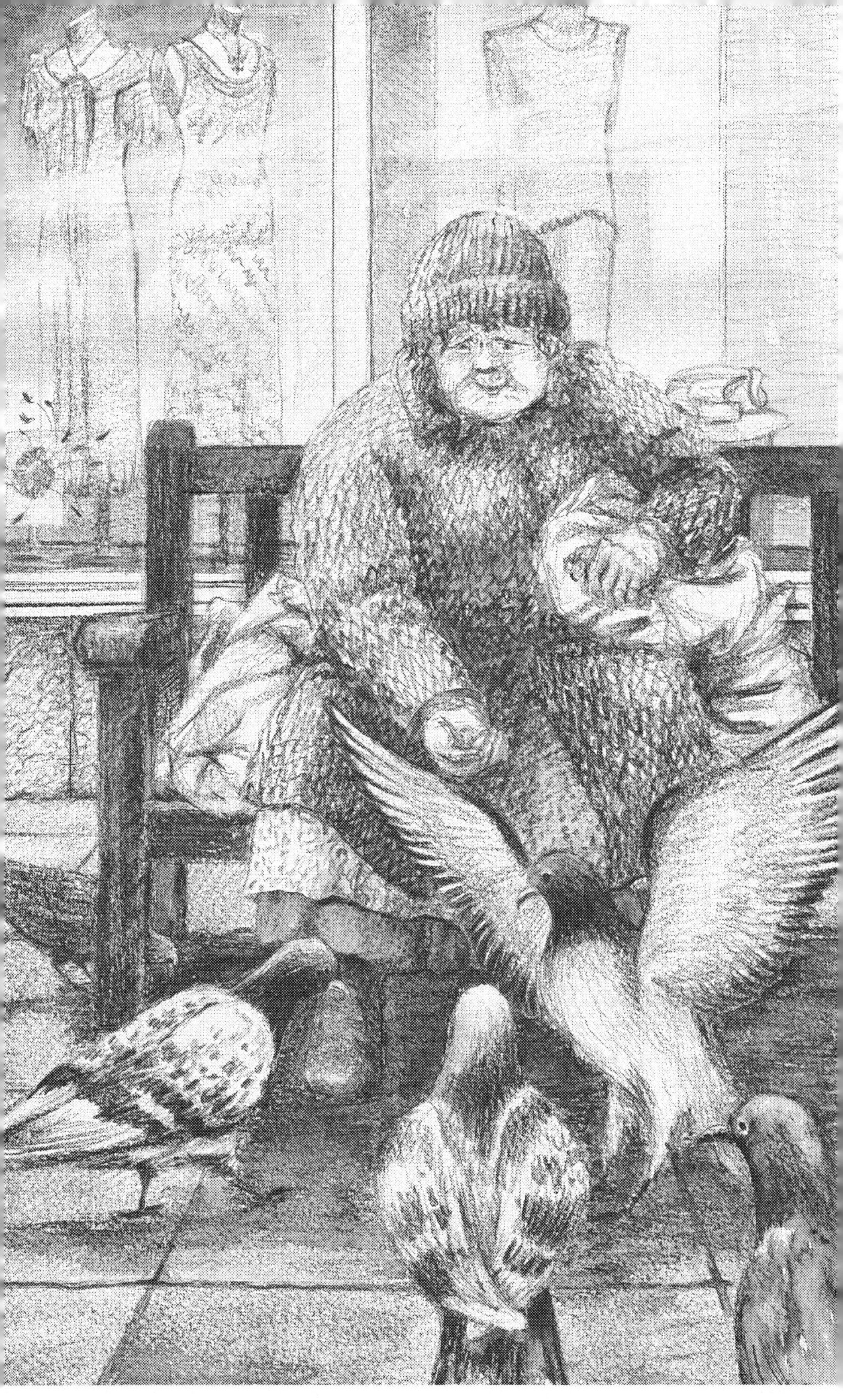

Shabby Goddess

Sissy feeds the pigeons
from a bench on The Strand.
She sits, bundled in strange layers,
to claim her place for the day.
Suited men and women pass
quickly and talk urgently to fill
their space with importance; girls
who glow with privilege through
their school uniforms slide
their eyes over her and away.

Sissy brings her bags each morning,
carefully sorted to soothe her reality;
bags of corn and wholemeal bread,
tasty gifts to sustain her faithful brood.
She knows each bird and names them,
pursing her lips to scold the bullying cocks,
cooing at the shyer ones. She grieves each
regular that doesn't appear at her feet,
and greets with joy any wanderer's return.

The afternoon wearies and Sissy gathers
herself, patting and fussing each carrier
bag in its turn. She squints at the sky,
whispers tenderly to birds that still
cluster around her and shuffles away;
back to a room somewhere no-one has seen.
Dipping and bowing, pigeons glean for last
morsels, then fly to their roosts on cornice
and roof. They wait for the morning
when the sun's rays will warm them,
and with it their shabby goddess will rise.

Sonnet for Women

My woman's cycle long since ceased to flow,
my body changed from lean to shape more round.
My hair, decreasing, in grey stripes does grow,
my spine sinks down and yearns for softer
ground.

The fount of motherhood has long been dry
and flesh once firm is texture of dead flowers.
The aches and pains of aging joints ask why
experience is spoiled by age that sours.

The moon now draws its tides to build internal
in tensile strength and belly deep connection
to lines of women, earth in life eternal
the force of roots, driving down to conception.

In age I spread, solid as continents;
sing blood, sing bone, till love's a monument

Small defences

I have not fought for this land;
I have not buckled on body armour
nor shouldered a gun.
I have not marched dusty roads
in formation, but I have walked,
with loving feet, its paths and trails
and I have grieved for its ancient trees
when greed makes war with concrete.

I have not sat in plane turret
or watchtower, scanning a misty
horizon for invaders and I have not
fought enemy hand to hand in the scent
of their sweat and blood.

But I have sat on a hilltop watching
over the slow rolling life of the valley
below and I have dug my fingers
into the soil to feel the stirring
of its loamy breath.

Strip the Willow

Strip the Willow, step a gyp and a hey
to shake our bells 'til the street rings with sound;
the hobby dips and bows, play fiddler, play!

Lads a Bunchem now boys, round as you may,
drive those feet down, wake the seeds in the ground.
Strip the Willow, step a gyp and a hey.

Can John or old Len jump higher today?
Remember the fool's wiser than he's found;
the hobby dips and bows, play fiddler, play!

Lets come, turn and kick to clash sticks and pray
that young Pete won't fall again on his round.
Strip the Willow, step a gyp and a hey.

To make the girls run, with a skip and a neigh,
clacking teeth to chase them up to the mound
the hobby dips and bows, play fiddler, play!

Lets dance, my lads, dance; send darkness away,
we leap for much more than colour display:
Strip the Willow, step a gyp and a hey,
the hobby dips and bows, play fiddler, play!

Springtime
(written in response to the 2001 Foot and Mouth outbreak)

Primroses are nestling under the hedge,
daffodils nod to each other in the breeze.
Sunlight dances dappling o'er the forest floor,
and new grass chokes under black drifts from the fire.

Young trees are blurred by soft green buds,
bees buzz their greetings to each new found flower.
Candy floss blossom offers its pledge to the year,
and char black legs plead skywards from the pyre.

Ewes murmur their chuckling song to their babes,
blackbird sings his heart for his love of this year.
Bright eyes blink from dens at new worlds to explore,
and white clad slaughtermen work their way through the byre.

They said she'd have to kiss a lot of frogs

She had been warned about the frogs,
and had braced herself for their wet kisses.
No-one mentioned the goats, or their rampant
delight in every sound and smell their hairy
bodies could make.

She hadn't been told of the lions: how they'd lie
in self-conscious beauty while they waited
for her to serve them, and how their roaring
for adoring attention could get on her nerves.

She wasn't prepared for the tom-cats and soon
tired of their expectations of a door left open,
bandages for their battle wounds and demands
for her lap when, rarely, they were home.

She read Sappho to help her forget the brief
incidents with gorillas and hyenas but when
she came to the warthog, her stoicism failed
and she moved in with the princess next door.

The Witch of Robinswood Hill

I don't know how long I have been dreaming
with the sound of the sap rising and falling around me.

The scent of woodsmoke still chokes, though it is long since I've drawn breath.

My sleep is always more fragile when the leaves
rustle as they curl and fall, and the squirrels scrabble
through the hollow to hide their stores.

The sounds of the season are too much like the crackle of flame.

The chatter of young voices scattered my rest;
I had to follow, drawn to the life in them
as if I had wings to singe on their lanterns.

When they came before, their torches flickered on faces twisted with fury and fear.

They led me over the hill while their guide
told stories to make them shriek and cling to each other.
I felt the lashes' sting with every tale.

Over long years anger drifts away like early mist, but this pain is beyond forgetting.

The trail led back, as I knew it must, to the tree where leafy
branches belie the charred heart; I don't know why it hurts
so, to listen to my life told as a legend.

The story lives beyond me, yet the flame still sears when I wake.

Tintagel

From a seamless edge where
    stacked slate melds
        into slate stacked cliff

at a place where sea
    booms under land

to watch a misty horizon
    where lights and shadows
        shift and shimmer

to feel my boundaries
    and defences
        dissolve.

Treesong

I would grow tall
cherishing knots and kinks
of experience.

I would mourn the loss
of every twig and bough
when winds of chance
bereave me, and fill
each new space with
green and vibrant leaf.

I would drive my roots down,
gently insistent on shifting
boulders and rocks from
my chosen way.

I would bend and split
with age:
reaching down to stroke
the earth, diffident
in querying its readiness
to receive me.

Town views

Headscarfed women nod
and chatter on the bus,
picking the coloured
bones of
others' lives.

Banners drape the Town Hall
telling of music for
the learned;
on the steps
skaters make their own.

Caryatids sulkily
lining the regency arcade
seem to cry for lack
of arms as petunias drip
from hanging baskets.

Iron pigeons crowning
fingerposts
don't make mess,
neither do they dance
in the street.

Alyssum and lobelias
sculpt time in the gardens,
used for short season and
thrown away; paper poppies
fade by the memorial stone.

Sale posters scream
red and orange from
shop windows while
the girl in the doorway
begs more quietly.

Children want at varied
volumes and scattered
tired mothers only
want holidays
to end.

The flower stall woman
'duck's and 'sweethearts'
through the day,
aging through years yet
never changing a word.

Shoppers and workers
are focussed and fast
while bright teenagers
bump hips and stroll
in the way.

The Big Issue seller's
pierced smile is gentle
as he greets each sale
and he fusses the blanket
for the dog at his feet.

In back streets buddleia
sprouts from cracked
concrete windowsills
and new kittens mew
from an abandoned car.

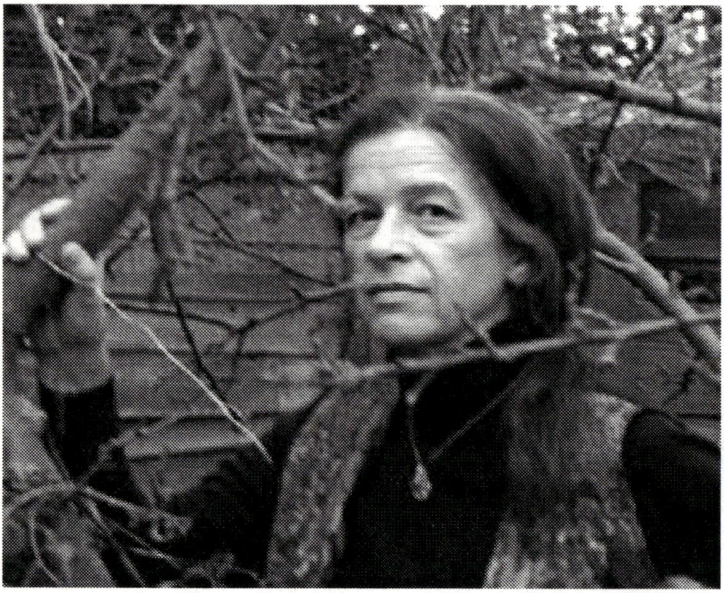

Angela France

Born in 1955 in Gloucestershire, England. She has travelled, and lived in different places, and is now back to Gloucestershire because of the strong connection she has for the particular corner of the land she loves.

Literature, in all its forms, has always been essential to her survival and she remains a voracious reader. Books are piled, shelved and boxed in every room of her house and she is constantly losing the contest of putting up shelves faster than acquiring books.

Angela started writing poetry at age 8, and was very prolific for a few years until teenage angst turned her writing darker than was fit for public consumption. Since then, life has taken over, and she only recently taken took up writing seriously again, as pure self indulgence.

She works with disadvantaged young people in various settings, whose resilience and spirit are constant inspirations. She lives with her teenage daughter, a cat, and a dog.

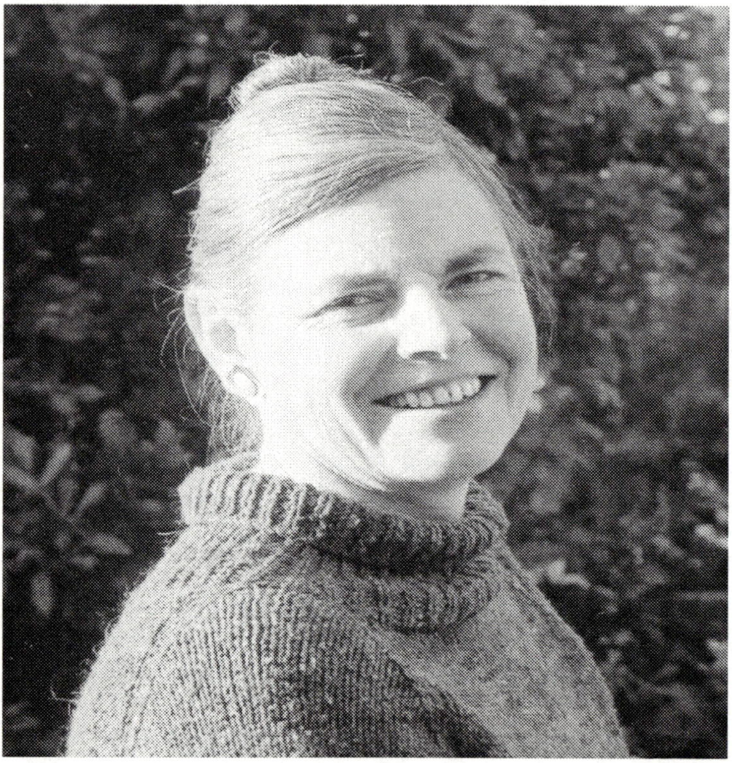

Elaine Blatchford

Attended Brighton and Manchester Colleges of Art studying graphics. She then worked in London and Germany before settling in Gloucestershire to bring up her family.

She likes working in pastels and drawing and is happy to be contacted through the publisher to accept commissions.

A pack of eight (8) postcards, one of each of her drawings together with part of the associated poem are available from the publisher.

Send a cheque for £4, post free
made payable to Author Publishing Ltd to:

   Author Publishing Ltd
   61 Gainsborough Road,
   Felixstowe, Suffolk,
   IP11 7HS, England